POPULAR
MISCONCEPTIONS

This edition printed in 2006 by

CHARTWELL BOOKS, INC.
A Division of BOOK SALES, INC.
114 Northfield Avenue
Edison, New Jersey 08837

ISBN-13: 978-0-7858-2172-4
ISBN-10: 0-7858-2172-4

Printed in China

CHARTWELL
BOOKS, INC.

Rumours, urban legends, word of mouth – there are a lot of so-called 'facts' out there that are simply not true. There are things that we think we know, but when we consider them more carefully, we find that we are not quite so sure after all. Misconceptions crop up in all areas of life, from geography to popular culture, history to the human body.

For example: Is the Great Wall of China the only man-made object that can be viewed from space? Do lemmings commit suicide by leaping off cliffs? Do men really think about sex every seven seconds?

Do you know the answers to these questions? Are you sure? Think again because this book is guaranteed to surprise you.

Popular misconceptions are things that none of us thinks we will ever be prey to, yet almost all of us are. Once you have read this compendium of myth-busters, you will be able to debunk any tall tales your friends try to pass as fact!

❓ INTRODUCTION

7

CURIOUS CREATURES

The animal kingdom is rich with facts that turn out to be oh-so-wrong. Birds and beasts, insects and lizards: none are safe from human misconceptions about their habits or habitats. Even dinosaurs cannot escape from the web of confusion we have spun over the years.

Spiders being swallowed, suicidal lemmings and sewer-dwelling alligators – they're all featured here but you might be rather surprised by what their real stories are. So it's time to stop burying your head in the sand (like ostriches do... don't they?) and discover the truth about the creepy crawlies and creatures that share our world.

CAN THE RICE THROWN AT WEDDINGS PROVE FATAL TO BIRDS?

More popular in the US than in the UK, the practice of throwing uncooked rice at a newly married couple has long been coupled with the myth that to do so poses a peril for our feathered friends. Columnist Ann Landers published advice in 1996 that stated that birds are in danger of exploding after eating uncooked rice that will then puff up in their teeny tummies.

The USA Rice Federation though was quick to inform Ms Landers: "This silly myth pops up periodically... Many migrating ducks and geese depend on winter-flooded rice fields each year to fatten up and build strength for their return trek to northern nesting grounds. Uncooked, milled rice is no more harmful to birds than rice in the field."

DO ALLIGATORS LIVE IN THE NEW YORK SEWER SYSTEM?

One of the most famous popular misconceptions of all time tells the tale of New Yorkers who bring baby alligators back from their Florida holidays and, when they have started to outgrow the 'cute' stage, flush them down the toilet. These alligators then thrive and grow in the sewers, living off rats and raw sewage.

Needless to say, it is entirely untrue. Not one sewer worker has ever reported seeing an alligator beneath the city, and there has never been a news story published about one. Also, alligators from Florida would have to live at a temperature far higher than can be found beneath New York.

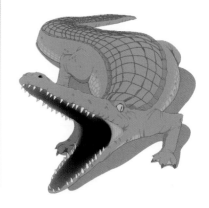

DO PENGUINS FALL OVER BACKWARDS WHILE WATCHING AEROPLANES FLYING OVERHEAD?

 DO LEMMINGS FREQUENTLY KILL THEMSELVES BY LEAPING OFF CLIFFS AND INTO THE SEA?

It's an amusing idea; thousands of penguins craning their necks to watch a plane flying overhead, then gently toppling over backwards like dominos when the plane passes over their heads. It does not happen outside of cartoons, though.

Such is the extent of the rumour that in November 2000, researchers spent a month looking at the 'falling penguin' phenomenon. Researcher Richard Stone summed up their findings: "Not one king penguin fell over when the helicopters came over Antarctic Bay. As the aircraft approached, the birds went quiet and… began walking away from the noise."

Despite being a 'fact' so famous and well established that a computer game was based on it, lemmings do not commit suicide by jumping off cliffs. In fact they don't commit suicide at all.

If there is competition between lemmings due to an explosion in population, or a lack of food, lemmings may migrate, and some may fall off cliffs during this process – due to being jostled in the rush – but it is not intentional 'suicide', just an accident. Lemmings will fight and kill each other rather than deliberately take their own lives.

? WHAT IS A CAMELHAIR BRUSH MADE FROM?

A paintbrush that one would assume is made from the hair of a camel is, rather confusingly, often made from almost every other animal except a camel, as camel hair is too woolly for brushes.

Whether they were ever made of camel hair is unknown, although that would explain their name. Animal hair used in camelhair brushes includes that of goats, squirrels, bears, ponies or sheep. It can also be a blend of more than one of these.

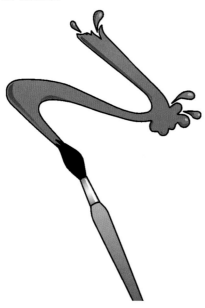

? WILL A MOTHER BIRD REJECT HER BABY IF THE CHICK IS HANDLED BY A HUMAN BEING?

Children are often told upon finding a fledgling on the ground that they should not pick it up because the mother bird will then smell human on it, and reject the poor chick. This is wrong – birds actually have a pretty terrible sense of smell.

That said, this popular misconception has been spread for the best of reasons – bird protection. After all, many people, when they see a baby bird out of its nest, want to return them to it or take the baby bird home. In reality, many hours are spent out of the nest while the fledgling is learning to fly so us humans should leave little birds well alone, as they are merely getting on with their growing up.

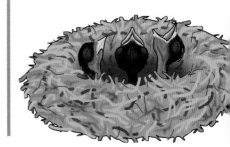

WHAT COLOUR IS A PURPLE FINCH?

Not purple, that's for sure. A male purple finch is much more red/crimson in colour, while the lady birdies are a brown-grey fleck, and they are similar to a sparrow in size. They are very popular with bird-watchers, as they will stay around a feeder for quite some time.

Purple finches usually nest in coniferous forests and build their nests with small twigs and fibres. Their eggs are green-blue with spots in black or brown and they usually lay about four or five. Quite why its name is so inaccurate is not clear.

IS THE DADDY LONGLEGS THE WORLD'S MOST POISONOUS CREATURE?

The common daddy longlegs is said to be the world's most poisonous insect, but does not pose a threat to humans, as its mouth is too small for it to bite us.

This is simply untrue. For one thing, the word poisonous implies it would do humans harm if we ate the insect; the word should be 'venomous'. And here there are also problems. In the UK, we refer to the crane fly as a daddy longlegs, and it is not venomous at all. Some spiders are also referred to as daddy longlegs – such as the pholcid spider – but there is no way of telling how venomous or poisonous they actually are.

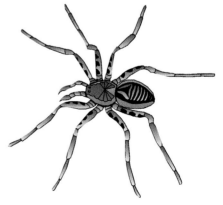

WHAT IS CATGUT MADE FROM?

The revolting-sounding catgut is a cord made from the intestines of animals. None of the animal guts used, however, are from a cat. The most commonly used animals for catgut are actually very unfeline-like sheep and horses!

Their intestines are stretched, then chemically treated and twisted together to form a strong cord. And if you managed to read that without feeling sick, then you will be delighted to know that catgut is used for stringing musical instruments – such as violins and harps, for some surgical sutures (although this is becoming much rarer) and for stringing tennis rackets.

ARE ELEPHANTS AFRAID OF MICE?

Although the cartoon image of a great elephant quivering atop a stool while a tiny mouse scurries beneath him is certainly amusing, it has absolutely no basis in fact.

Elephants are very brave creatures. They also have terrible eyesight, and so are unlikely to see a mouse, much less be scared by one. It is possible that this rumour sprung up because elephants may show distress if there is a movement nearby that they cannot identify – but it is more likely that the idea of something so big being scared of something so small is such a delicious study in contrasts that it tickles our collective funny bone.

❓ ARE PIRANHAS A DANGEROUS, MAN-EATING FISH?

While not cuddly little pets, stories of schools of piranhas attacking live humans and stripping their flesh down to the bone are exaggerated. In most of the cases reported, the human was already dead from other causes before the fish attacked.

However, they are vicious and will bite people, especially to defend their brood. This happens more in dammed rivers, as there is a larger build-up of numbers there. Piranhas generally live in South American rivers and lakes and are carnivores, feeding off other fish and – occasionally – a nibble on a human leg!

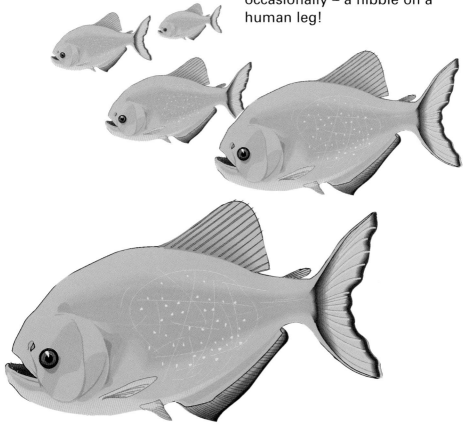

DO CHAMELEONS CHANGE COLOUR TO MATCH THEIR SURROUNDINGS?

Chameleons do not change colour to match or blend in with their surroundings. This myth has probably arisen from the fact that chameleons can change colour, coupled with the fact that they are usually difficult to spot when in their natural environment.

Importantly though, they change colour when their mood changes, rather than as camouflage. Chameleons are normally a green-brown colour and have a slow walk that seems to mimic a leaf being blown in the wind. They also stay still for very long periods of time, which can make them very difficult to spot.

DO OSTRICHES BURY THEIR HEADS IN THE SAND?

This myth is so famous that people are warned not to 'bury their heads in the sand' meaning not to ignore possible danger signs. This cliché is based on the presumption – encouraged by cartoons – that an ostrich will bury its head in the sand when threatened, leaving its body on display to any predator.

However, this is not what ostriches actually do – when scared or threatened, ostriches put their head and neck on the ground. When seen from a distance, this may look as if their heads are buried beneath the sand, as their head and neck are lighter in colour and would blend with the sand, while their darker bodies would stand out. At no point, does the ostrich actually stick its head in the sand!

DO TOADS GIVE YOU WARTS?

 ## DO CATS ALWAYS FALL ON THEIR FEET?

The warty appearance of a toad's skin has given rise to the entirely false assumption that touching a toad will give you warts. This is false as the warts on a toad are not an infection that can be passed on.

Warts in humans are caused when germs enter the skin and cause cells to reproduce rapidly, leading to a small growth.

Although humans can pass warts to each other, this is unlikely as they are only mildly infectious. Toads, however, are totally blame-free.

Strangely enough, when falling from a very small distance, a cat may not land on its feet, as it will not have the time to turn the right way up for this to happen.

However, the ability to 'right' itself in the air means that cats can fall a long way and come away relatively unscathed.

One study proved that cats that fell fewer than seven storeys were more injured than cats that fell further. This study concluded that the animals spread themselves, like a flying squirrel, when falling from greater heights and thus prevented serious injury.

However, as this survey was based on injured cats, it did not take into account the number of cats that may not have survived a fall of a height greater than seven storeys.

DOES THE AVERAGE PERSON REALLY SWALLOW EIGHT SPIDERS PER YEAR?

Not only is this entirely untrue, but it was deliberately spread as a rumour to see what people will believe when they are sent information by e-mail.

In a 1993 article for *PC Professional* magazine, Lisa Holst wrote about how truly gullible people were when it came to information gleaned from the internet.

She compiled a list of things that were not true – including the 'fact' about swallowing eight spiders a year – and circulated it by e-mail all over the internet.

As people are still stating it as fact today without ever bothering to check its origins, we think Holst proved her point really rather well.

IS RAT URINE DEADLY TO HUMANS?

In the late-1990s, scare stories began circulating on the internet about people who had died after drinking straight from a drinks can.

The reason for their demise was given as rat urine on the can, which – said the e-mails – was lethal to human beings. Some e-mails also warned that rat faeces, when dry, could form a powder and have the same effect. As many cans are stored in warehouses, where rats may be, this was quite a story. It was, however, not a true story. No one has died after drinking from a can that has been tainted with rat urine. In fact, the urine or faeces from a healthy rat would do humans no harm; only if the rat was ill is there a remote possibility of disease – but it would certainly not be carried by drinks cans.

WILL IGUANAS ONLY GROW TO THE SIZE OF THEIR CAGE?

An argument frequently used by children trying to get an iguana as a pet is that it will only grow to the size of its cage, implying that the iguana will be no trouble as it will not get too big or need rehousing.

As many parents who fell for this have discovered, this 'fact' is simply not true. As long as they are well fed and properly cared for, there is no reason why an iguana shouldn't grow up to five or six ft in length. And as it is recommended that an iguana enclosure should be at least twice the length of an iguana, this is certainly not a low-maintenance pet!

 ARE CATS DANGEROUS TO PREGNANT WOMEN?

Doctors used to tell women that if they were living with a cat then it was best to get rid of the animal, as it could prove harmful to their pregnancy. This is a confusion of the facts.

What is worrisome for pregnant women is the link between cats and the parasitic disease Toxoplasmosis, which can be dangerous to an unborn baby. However, this can only be passed on by handling the cat's faeces and so, as long as she stays away from this charming task – and anything associated with the litter tray – then there is no reason why a pregnant woman and her cat can't happily cohabit.

? DID THE TYRANNOSAURUS REX LIVE IN THE JURASSIC PERIOD?

Ever since the blockbuster movie _Jurassic Park_, people have been able to name a period in dinosaur history, even if they know nothing about the creatures themselves.

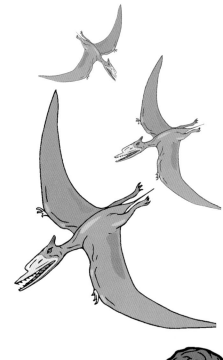

The fact is that the mighty Tyrannosaurus Rex did not live in the Jurassic period, but rather in the Cretaceous period. As a guide, the Jurassic period began about 210 million years ago and lasted for 70 million years, while the Cretaceous period began about 85 million years ago and lasted for roughly 20 million years. Also, the Tyrannosaurus Rex was not necessarily green. Although often portrayed in this fetching shade, it is simply an educated guess. No one knows what colour the T Rex was. Not even Mr Steven Spielberg.

FUN FOOD & DAFT DRINKS

Aside from keeping us alive and tasting pretty great, food also appears to have another purpose – namely to be the focus of popular misconceptions buzzing around out there. From brand names like Heinz and Coca-Cola, to old wives' tales and urban legends, this section will certainly give you food for thought.

Do you frequently tap the top of a fizzy drinks can to stop it foaming over? Or eat carrots to help improve your night vision? Or drink eight glasses of water a day to keep from becoming dehydrated? Then prepare to be surprised by the information in this section. And remember to take the food 'facts' you hear in the future with a large pinch of salt!

WHY DID HEINZ ADOPT THE SLOGAN '57 VARIETIES'?

Most people think that the globally successful HJ Heinz company took up using the slogan '57 varieties' because their production line at the time made 57 different products.

However, by 1896 – when founder Henry James Heinz came up with the slogan – the Heinz production line contained over 60 items and was rapidly expanding. The story behind the slogan is that Heinz saw an advert promising '21 styles of shoe'. Being a clever man, he realised that an advertising slogan needed to be catchy, so he came up with '57 varieties' which, although catchy, was essentially meaningless.

DID A COCA-COLA AD CAMPAIGN REALLY CREATE THE MODERN IMAGE OF SANTA CLAUS?

The evolution and creation of the modern image of Santa Claus – jolly man, red and white suit, flying reindeer, etc. – has been a long and complicated process.

Yet many believe that it was down to the Coca-Cola advertising campaigns of the 1930s. Although these campaigns may have helped to cement this particular image of Santa in the public consciousness, a red-suited Santa can be found on Christmas cards as early as 1885, and a 1927 article in the *New York Times* refers to "a standardized Santa Claus," with "red garments… and the white whiskers."

DOES DROPPED FOOD REMAIN GERM-FREE AS LONG AS YOU PICK IT UP WITHIN FIVE SECONDS?

WILL TAPPING THE SIDE OF A FIZZY DRINKS CAN PREVENT IT FROM FOAMING OVER WHEN OPENED?

A favourite of frustrated mothers everywhere, the 'five-second rule' that food will remain germ-free after being dropped on the floor, provided it is picked up within five seconds, is sadly not true.

Viruses and bacteria attach themselves to food on contact, so the length of time spent in contact with them is irrelevant. And, as no floor is guaranteed clean – all sorts of nasties come in on the soles of our shoes or feet – once the food hits the floor, the possibility of infection is there. And, although some viruses and bacteria will have little or no effect, there are also those that can make us seriously ill.

It's another famous example of word of mouth triumphing over scientific fact. The only reason why tapping the side or top of a drinks can will prevent the foam-over is that it takes a little longer than opening the can immediately; and it is *time* that calms the bubbles, rather than the actual tapping action.

The 'fizz' in a can is caused by a process combining carbon dioxide and water together under pressure. Opening the can releases this pressure, and causes bubbles of gas to form in the liquid and rise to the surface. The can will foam over when it has been jostled or shaken as this creates more bubbles to overflow when the pressure is released. Tapping the can will do nothing to prevent this, although just allowing time to pass will allow carbon dioxide to be reabsorbed into the liquid.

WILL A TOOTH DISSOLVE IF LEFT IN A GLASS OF COCA-COLA OVERNIGHT?

It's a tooth–rotting, stomach–churning idea. If leaving a tooth in a glass of Coca-Cola overnight will cause it to dissolve, then what awful damage will drinking it do to your own teeth and what harm will come to your poor tummy and intestines?

To start at the beginning, a tooth left in a glass of Coca-Cola overnight will not completely dissolve; it will actually begin to dissolve after a couple of days.

However, the acids in Coca-Cola that can dissolve a tooth if given long enough – such as citric acid and phosphoric acid – are also present in beverages such as orange juice. Thankfully though, our stomachs are more than equipped to deal with them.

 WILL EATING CARROTS MAKE YOU ABLE TO SEE IN THE DARK?

Or improve your eyesight? No, not really, although there is a little bit of science to back up this commonly held misconception.

Carrots are a rich source of beta-carotene, which can help slow the eye's degeneration. However, it is hard to say how many carrots would have to be eaten to gain the levels needed to slow down deteriorating eyesight. And a diet consisting of a lot of carrots is not recommended as they are also high in Vitamin A, which should not be consumed in high quantities. However, for sufferers of nyctalopia (night–blindness, or difficulty seeing in poor light), eating more carrots can make a difference.

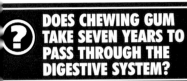

DOES CHEWING GUM TAKE SEVEN YEARS TO PASS THROUGH THE DIGESTIVE SYSTEM?

A favourite of parents everywhere in an attempt to stop their children swallowing something that – essentially – is not food, this is nevertheless, quite untrue.

Although chewing gum is not intended to be swallowed, it will still take the same amount of time to pass from one end of a human being to the other. The claim that it will sit in your stomach for years may come from the fact that chewing gum is indigestible. However, this simply means that the body does not break chewing gum down the way it does with other foodstuffs. Hence, the gum will pass through the digestive system without changing form very much – but it will pass through and not stick anywhere it shouldn't.

WHERE DOES GERMAN CHOCOLATE CAKE COME FROM?

This hugely popular dessert is often assumed to have originated in Germany; however, the 'German' of the title is actually the name of an American baker whose creations made the recipe possible.

In 1852, a 'sweet baking bar' was created for Baker's Chocolate Company by a man called Sam German, and was named Baker's German's Sweet Chocolate. When it was used as an ingredient in recipes, the apostrophes were often missed out, leading to the confusion.

The very first recipe for German Chocolate Cake was published in 1957, which lead to a massive increase in sales of German Sweet Chocolate and the launch of an enduring dessert favourite.

IS CAESAR SALAD NAMED AFTER JULIUS CAESAR?

Almost everyone, if asked, will presume that Caesar salad was either created by or named after Julius Caesar. But almost everyone would be totally wrong. Not only is it nothing to do with Julius Caesar, but it also has nothing to do with any of the Caesars that ran the Roman empire.

The dish is, in fact, named after its creator, Caesar Cardini, who invented it in Mexico in 1924. Although the original recipe contained many of the ingredients we know today, it was missing anchovies, as Cardini is said to have been against their inclusion, believing that the tangy Worcestershire sauce provided enough of the fish flavour.

 WILL BANANAS BE EXTINCT WITHIN 15 YEARS?

A couple of years back, scaremongers began circulating the story that a combination of a leaf fungus and a soil fungus would lead to the extinction of the humble banana within 15 years. These claims were even published in *New Scientist*, which only gave bananas 10 years.

However, not only have these claims now been refuted, but it turns out they were only referring to one type of banana – out of over 300 different types available – the Cavendish banana. This is the most popular type of banana in the West, and is under threat from Panama Disease (otherwise known as Race 4). However, there will be bananas in our fruit bowls for a long time yet. Unless they are wiped out by Race Beta 45. Only kidding…

WHERE DOES SAUERKRAUT COME FROM?

Due to its name, many assume that sauerkraut (or sour cabbage) originates in Germany. As with German Chocolate Cake, the name is misleading.

Sauerkraut was certainly known and eaten by the Romans – who added salt and vinegar to their cabbage to make it last longer.

It is presumed that the improvement in its preparation was created in Germany in the Middle Ages, and it became so popular there that people believed that it must have originated from the land of the Hun.

WILL YOU BECOME DEHYDRATED IF YOU DRINK LESS THAN EIGHT GLASSES OF WATER A DAY?

Although this is generally accepted as a rule, no-one is really sure where the figure of 'eight glasses' actually came from.

Generally, to remain healthy, the human body needs to replace the water it has lost throughout the day. Kidney physiologist Jurgen Schnermann was quoted in the *Los Angeles Times* as saying "an average-sized adult with healthy kidneys sitting in a temperate climate needs no more than one litre of fluid." This is about the same amount of water the average adult gets from their solid food.

Although drinking water is recommended by health experts, there really won't be any horrific consequences if you drink less than the magic 'eight glasses'. So you can take a deep breath and relax now...

PURE
SPRING
WATER
340ml

ARE BROWN EGGS HEALTHIER THAN WHITE EGGS?

Perhaps the confusion over this one stems from brown and white bread, or brown and white sugar? But the truth of the matter is that there is no nutritional difference between brown and white eggs.

According to the Egg Nutrition Center in America, white eggs come from white hens and brown eggs come from red hens. You can also get speckled eggs from chickens, and light blue ones, and these are also nutritionally exactly the same as white and brown eggs are – and they all taste the same as well!

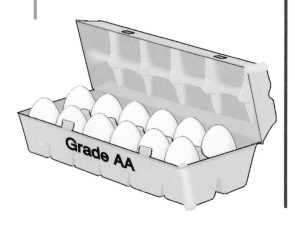

Grade AA

 DOES THE 'HAIR OF THE DOG' REMEDY WORK TO CURE A HANGOVER?

When you actually discover the origins for this saying, it i no surprise to find that it doe not work. In ancient times, th advice was to put a hair of th dog that bit you on the woun to make it heal quicker.

This did not work, and neithe does drinking more alcohol to rid yourself of a hangover. Your body needs time to repa the damage done by drinking The reason drinking again ma make you feel better is that you will be going back to the nice stage of drinking – wher everything feels good.

However, you are not 'curir your hangover, merely puttin it off. Sadly, the only 'cure' guaranteed to prevent a hangover is not drinking too much in the first place.

DOES BLACK COFFEE SOBER UP SOMEONE WHO IS DRUNK?

We've all seen it in the movies, but in reality, the only way to sober someone up is to wait until their liver has got rid of the alcohol from their system. Coffee may perk up a sleepy drunk, but it cannot make the liver do its job any faster.

And because the only thing that can sober someone up is time itself, this also means that other urban myths are incorrect; a cold shower will not work (and could even put someone into shock), neither will making someone throw up (as alcohol is absorbed into the blood stream).

Sleeping will not help either, although it often seems effective as a way of passing the time needed for the liver to do its job.

DOES GREEN TEA INCREASE A WOMAN'S FERTILITY?

A fairly new urban legend has sprung up around women who are trying to conceive. The myth is that drinking green tea will somehow make them more fertile, and conception will happen quicker. Alas, there is no scientific proof that green tea affects fertility in any way.

However, green tea does contain caffeine and tannic acid, both of which are linked to fertility problems and an increased risk of miscarriage.

It is certainly not worth steering clear of green tea, as the amounts are far lower than in black tea or coffee, but it is curious that such a rumour has grown over green tea specifically.

IS CHOCOLATE BAD FOR YOU?

Long blamed for everything from obesity to spots, chocolate has had a bad reputation for too long. The fact is that – in moderation, and as part of a balanced diet – chocolate can even be beneficial. And it doesn't cause spots.

Dark chocolate is the best for you as it helps increase the body's levels of HDL, a type of cholesterol that helps prevent fat blocking the arteries. A scientist in California, Profession Carl Keen, created quite a stir when he suggested that chocolate could help prevent heart disease due to the flavonoids it contains, which thin the blood and help prevent clotting. Further research is being carried out, but it is worth mentioning that Keen's research was funded by mega-confectioner Mars...

HOPELESS HISTORIES & DUBIOUS DATES

History seems like a subject that should not be as prone to misconceptions as some others. After all, it is factually-based – these things really happened – so why are there still so many inaccuracies floating about? Word of mouth, it seems, is often the culprit, aided by inaccurate history books, biased memories – and some people who just get things wrong but sound convincing.

From Titanic travesties to Biblical blunders, this chapter trawls through the past to dig up troublesome rumours and finally set the record straight.

So, if you really thought Tutankhamen's tomb was cursed or that Vikings wore horned helmets, then prepare to have your perceptions altered!

DID THE TITANIC CARRY A CURSED MUMMY ONBOARD?

For many years a story has done the rounds about the curse of the Princess Amen-Ra, a mummy who caused death and destruction to those that discovered her, owned and transported her.

The tale ends with the mummy being carried onboard the Titanic, and therefore being to blame for the ship's unfortunate end. As with all great ghost stories, this one is not true.
  The cargo manifest for the Titanic shows no mummies at all. And for the record, the Princess of Amen-Ra is actually just a coffin lid, not an actual mummy, and never left the British Museum, let alone took a transatlantic trip aboard the Titanic!

WAS THE TITANIC THE FIRST SHIP TO USE THE SOS DISTRESS CALL?

According to legend, the Titanic's senior wireless operator Jack Phillips stayed at his post until the last minute, going down with the ship in his effort to save the day. And in doing so, he was the first to use the SOS distress call.

The SOS call had been chosen at the 1906 International Conference of Wireless Communication at Sea because of its dot–dot–dot dash–dash–dash dot–dot–dot Morse code, and not because the initials stood for anything. Previous to this people in Britain had used the letters CQD. Phillips used both the old CQD and the new SOS, but he was not the first to do so. Ships such as Araphoe (1909), Kentucky (1910), Merida and Niobe (both 1911) had already been recorded as using the new distress call.

IN WHAT MONTH DO RUSSIANS CELEBRATE THE OCTOBER REVOLUTION?

Strangely enough, the Russians actually celebrate the famous October Revolution in November.

When Bolshevik leader Vladimir Lenin led his leftist revolutionaries in an uprising in Petrograd, the then capital of Russia, it was October 25, 1917, according to the Julian calendar that was still used in Russia at the time. However, according to the current Gregorian calendar, the date was November 7. Also, the revolution was bloodless for the most part, despite later depictions by the Soviet Union.

HOW LONG DID THE 100 YEARS WAR LAST?

Often used as a trick question, the 100 Years War between England and France actually lasted for a total of 116 years, beginning in 1337 and ending in 1453.

The ridiculously long war saw such events as the 1381 Peasant's Revolt, the taking of Calais by the English and the burning of Joan of Arc as a witch.

It was also not really one long war, but more a series of conflicts between the English and the French that historians have grouped together and labelled the 100 Years War.

DID NOSTRADAMUS PREDICT THE 9/11 TERRORIST ACTS?

Shortly after the attacks on the World Trade Center and the Pentagon in 2001, an e-mail began circulating, featuring the following quote: "In the City of God there will be a great thunder, two brothers torn apart by chaos, while the fortress endures, the great leader will succumb. The third big war will begin when the big city is burning on the 11th day of the 9th month that... two metal birds would crash into two tall statues in the new city and the world will end soon after."

The quote was attributed to Nostradamus, writing in 1654. However, nowhere in the writings of Nostradamus does this quote appear, nor does any reference to the 9/11 events ever appear.

DID MARY RIDE A DONKEY TO BETHLEHEM?

Thousands of nativity plays can't be wrong... can they? Actually, the Bible never mentions that Mary rode a donkey to Bethlehem; in fact it doesn't mention how she got there at all, only that she went there with Joseph.

There is also no mention of her arriving at the inn on the day she gave birth, or that either Mary or Joseph spoke with any innkeepers. It is far more likely that they stayed in a stable behind someone's house, rather than behind a Bible–era hotel. Oh, and there is nothing that says Jesus was born in a stable – just that he was laid in a manger, as there was no other space for him.

DID EVE GIVE ADAM AN APPLE?

According to the Bible story, Eve ate from the Tree of the Knowledge of Good and Evil, and then brought some of the fruit to Adam, who also ate it.

As God had forbidden them to eat the fruit of this tree, this disobedience led to human beings being cast out of the Garden of Eden, having to endure the wearing of clothes, and experience huge pain during childbirth.

However, nowhere in the Bible does it ever say that the fruit from the Tree of the Knowledge of Good and Evil is an apple. In some other cultures, it is actually said to be a fig tree.

DID MARIE ANTOINETTE SAY: "LET THEM EAT CAKE"?

It seems very unlikely that this quote comes from Marie Antoinette. When her husband Louis XVI was crowned in 1774, it was at the height of a bread shortage in Paris. Marie Antoinette is then said to have joked: "Qu'ils mangent de la brioche" ("[If they have no bread,] then let them eat cake"). While sources vary for the origin of the quote, it was not Antoinette who said it.

The renowned philosopher of the time, Jean-Jacques Rousseau, wrote: "Finally, I remembered the way out suggested by a great princess when told the peasants had no bread: 'Well, let them eat cake'," but Rousseau was not speaking about Antoinette. It is possible that Maria Theresa of Spain, an earlier French queen, actually spoke those famous words.

DID ISAAC NEWTON INVENT GRAVITY?

A common misuse of words – Isaac Newton did not invent gravity because as we know, gravity has always been with us! What Newton did was observe gravity and attempt to explain how the force of gravity acts upon matter within our universe.

It is said that Newton was led to pursue the idea of gravity when an apple fell from a tree and hit him on the head. Probably after checking that it wasn't children playing a joke, he went on to contemplate whether the force that had made the apple fall was the same one that kept the moon orbiting the earth.

Thus began the heady investigation into the quantification of gravity.

HOW MANY ENGLISH KINGS WERE CALLED ALBERT?

A quick glance at the history books would seem to indicate that there has never been a king of England with the name Albert – but there have actually been two.

Queen Victoria's husband, Albert, was Prince Consort, and it was her wish upon his death that no future king should ever be called Albert.

Therefore, when Victoria's eldest son Albert Edward succeeded to the throne, he went by the name Edward VII. His eldest son Albert died before becoming king, so George V succeeded Edward.

His second son was born on December 14, 1895, which was the anniversary of the death of the Prince Consort. In tribute, the child was called Albert Frederick Arthur George but Albert actually took the throne with the name George VI.

WAS THE SPANISH INQUISITION A BRUTAL AND FANATICAL TIME OF TORTURE AND MURDER?

"No one expects the Spanish Inquisition!" It is certainly a time that has passed into infamy as one of brutal torture, religious fanaticism and murder most horrid… but is that really the case?

Not according to many historians and a team of 30 scholars who were invited by the Vatican to look through the archives of the Holy Office in 1998. What they found was then published in an 800-page report that surprised many. Torture during the Spanish Inquisition was rare, and only 1% of those brought before the Inquisition accused of heresy were ever executed – most were actually acquitted or received suspended sentences, thus saving them from bloody vigilante justice.

When the 'witch hunt' spread across Europe, it was places with established Inquisitions that found women accused of witchcraft innocent. In other places, they were put to death by drowning or burning.

DID MUSSOLINI MAKE THE TRAINS RUN ON TIME?

After Benito Mussolini was appointed prime minister of Italy in 1922, he needed a way to convince the Italian public that fascism was a good system that would benefit them, so he used the trains to illustrate this.

It soon became common knowledge that in Mussolini's Italy, the trains ran on time, and people still believe it today. However, the majority of the improvements to Italy's railways actually took place *before* Mussolini came to power in 1922. Also, some who lived in Italy during that era claim that the 'perfect' timekeeping was nowhere near as good as it was reported as being.

 WAS TUTANKHAMEN'S TOMB CURSED?

When the tomb of Tutankhamen was discovered in 1923, one newspaper reported that there was a curse written in hieroglyphics at the entrance, which read: "They who enter this sacred tomb shall be visited by wings of death." However, the written curse did not exist.

Many still seem to believe though that those who dared enter the ancient tomb of Tutankhamen met untimely deaths. However, many of the team lived on to see old age, including Howard Carter, who discovered the tomb and spent ten years working in it. He died 17 years after discovering the tomb, at the age of 64. Dr DE Derry, who carried out the autopsy on Tutankhamen's mummy, didn't die until 1969.

DID CHASTITY BELTS EVER REALLY EXIST?

DID VIKINGS HAVE HORNS ON THEIR HELMETS?

Apparently not, according to a report in *The Sunday Times* and several prominent historians. They believe that chastity belts were most likely a Victorian myth, and those that do exist were manufactured in the 19th century as curiosities or jokes.

Prior to this, chastity belts were believed to have been invented in the Middle Ages to stop women engaging in sexual intercourse. Historian James Brundage dismisses this theory: "It is unlikely belts were anything more than a handy gag for burlesque writers." Felicity Riddy, of the Centre for Medieval Studies at York University, agrees, saying: "It all points to an early urban myth brought back to life by the Victorians."

The image of marauding and savage Vikings would not be complete without the image of their horned helmets set atop their long locks, so it will be a surprise to many to find out that it is extremely unlikely that Vikings ever had horns on their helmets.

The only historical evidence of horned helmets comes from crests that have been found, but not one of them dates from the era of the Scandinavian raids that happened between the late-8th and late-11th centuries. In fact, Viking helmets were either conical or hemispherical in shape, and some would even have had face protectors attached to them. Those Vikings, eh? Not quite so butch after all...

WERE SUITS OF ARMOUR SO HEAVY THAT WEARERS COULD BARELY MOVE AND NEEDED HELP GETTING ON TO THEIR HORSES?

The image of a knight having to be helped on to his horse, or a suit of armour being so heavy that it takes several men to carry it are popular ones in films and television shows, but they are entirely false.

A suit of armour used in battle would usually weigh between 45 and 55lb, with a 4–8lb helmet. This is less than modern soldiers carry into battle, and less than a fireman's uniform complete with oxygen gear.

Armour did increase in weight when firearms became popular, but then it was usually only in the torso area, rather than the full-body armour.

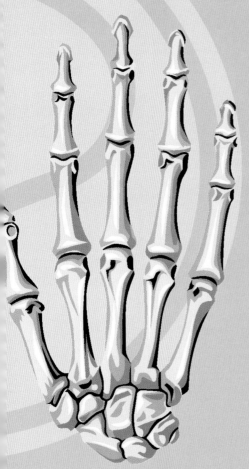

HUMAN BODY BITS & PIECES

Despite the fact that we all have one and use it every day of our lives, most of us have very little idea about what makes the human body actually work. This lack of knowledge has led to many misconceptions.

It seems there is barely an inch of flesh that has not had rumours circulating about it.

Will a sudden shock turn your hair white? Do your fingernails continue to grow after your death? And does hair grow back thicker once it has been shaved? What do you think? Perhaps all these rumours catch on simply because we are all only using 10% of our brains. Or are we?

There has been a story circulating on the internet and through e-mails for several years now. In it, a businessman is drugged and unconscious until he wakes up in a bath full of ice, with a phone by his side and instructions to ring an ambulance if he wants to live. Upon receiving medical assistance, it is discovered his kidneys have been stolen!

This urban legend became such a popular tale that in 1997, the New Orleans Police Department received over 100 telephone calls from the concerned public, leading them to make the statement that the stories were "without merit and foundation. The warnings that are disseminated through the internet are fictitious."

Although it can appear that way, hair does not grow back any thicker once it has been shaved. The reason that it loo and feels that way is twofold. One reason is that long hair feels softer than short hair – much like a bamboo cane is flexible when long, but stiff when cut short.

Also, when longer hair is not c off, the ends become naturally tapered, and therefore thinner than at the base of the hair. Shaving will expose this thick base of the hair – although it will become naturally tapered left to grow again. And while we're on the subject – plucking out one grey hair will not caus two to grow in its place. Although, in the months it tak to grow another hair, you may have more grey hairs than yo had before.

In the not-too-distant past, women who suspected they might be with child had to provide their doctor with a urine sample and wait while that sample was subjected to the 'rabbit test'. This involved the urine being injected into a rabbit, as it had been discovered that the hormone present in the urine of pregnant women would result in distinct ovarian changes in a rabbit.

Often on TV, a positive result was announced with the news "the rabbit died" leading many to believe that the rabbit died during testing. However, although in the early days all the rabbits died (as that was the only way to examine their ovaries), it was soon discovered that the changes could be observed without the bunny buying it...

Although it is unlikely that you could fall pregnant while nursing a baby, it is still possible – a fact not known to many, and therefore responsible for more than a few surprises!

Breastfeeding means the body produces less of the hormone needed for ovulation, so a woman's chances of conceiving while exclusively breastfeeding her infant are much lower than usual. It is still possible, however, although unlikely. But what many women fail to realize is that mixing breastfeeding with occasional bottles of formula milk or weaning their baby on to solid food, could be all it takes for their bodies to start producing the hormone again.

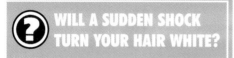

WILL A SUDDEN SHOCK TURN YOUR HAIR WHITE?

This has never been proven, and if it appears to have happened then the most likely explanation is coincidence.

People usually go grey or white slowly but for some, the process happens quicker, often aided by hair loss conditions, which cause the coloured hair to fall out and leave only the grey or white hairs behind.

Certainly the hair already on your head cannot change colour as this is dead hair so it is the hair growing through underneath that would be white. However, attributing the seemingly sudden colour change to a shock or fright is nothing new. Lord Byron wrote in 1816: "My hair is grey, but not with years,/ Nor grew it white/ In a single night/ As men's have grown from sudden fears."

DO WE USE ONLY 10% OF OUR BRAINS?

This is another widely-stated 'fact' that is completely false, as we use pretty much all of our brain, although not all the time. It is unclear where this myth started, although it has certainly been leapt upon by psychics and those who deal with the unexplained.

A good example of this is the psychic Uri Geller, who claims in the introduction to *Uri Geller's Mind–Power Book*, "most of us only use about 10% of our brains. The other 90% is full of untapped potential and undiscovered abilities, which means our minds are only operating in a very limited way instead of at full stretch."

The truth is although a simple task, such as brushing our teeth, may only take up a small percentage of our brain's power, we will use more as the day progresses and as we participate in more and more tasks.

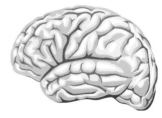

DO A PERSON'S FINGERNAILS AND HAIR CONTINUE TO GROW AFTER DEATH?

DO YOU RISK DROWNING IF YOU GO SWIMMING AFTER LUNCH?

It's a widely held popular misconception that once we shuffle off this mortal coil, our hair and nails continue to grow even though we are dearly departed.

Alas, this ghoulish image is the stuff of nonsense – what's actually happening is that the skin round the nails and hair is simply drying up and retracting, creating the illusion that the nails and hair are growing. Never has the phrase "too much information" been quite so true.

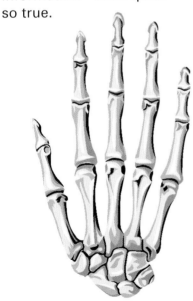

Some people believe that going for a swim after gorging on food is a bad idea because it could lead to drowning by stomach cramps.

The paranoia-inducing advice states that children in particular must wait an hour before daring to go for a doggy paddle. In actual fact, there is no recorded death-by-drowning associated with stomach cramps caused by stuffing your face. In fact, you've more chance of being eaten by a Great White than suffering death-by-undigested-sarnie.

IF YOU DREAM YOU ARE FALLING, WILL YOU DIE IF YOU HIT THE FLOOR?

Dreaming that you are plummeting to your death often results in a sudden, sharp awakening, seconds before you hit the floor.

Another similar dream is one in which you trip and, again, awaken just before hitting the floor. These dreams are so common that an urban legend has sprung up around them, namely that if you were to hit the ground in your dream, then you would die in your sleep.

Although impossible to prove one way or the other, this legend has no basis in fact. However, a dream about falling is said to represent a feeling of being overwhelmed and out of control in your day-to-day life, or possibly represent a sense of failure.

DO HAEMOPHILIACS BLEED TO DEATH?

Haemophilia is a disease that affects the body's ability to clot blood. The common misconception about haemophiliacs is that they will bleed to death from a scratch or a wound.

Writing about the subject for *FDA Consumer* magazine, Ken Flieger says: "External bleeding is seldom a serious problem for haemophiliacs. They may bleed somewhat longer than other people, but minor bleeding episodes can generally be controlled by ordinary first-aid measures. On the other hand, unchecked internal bleeding can be serious – even life-threatening – for a person with haemophilia."

The most common kind of internal bleeding is called spontaneous bleeding, and mainly affects the joints – knees, elbows, shoulders, ankles, wrists and hips – which will swell up when affected.

DO MEN THINK ABOUT SEX EVERY SEVEN SECONDS?

Or every six seconds? Although the time frame often varies (sometimes stretching to as long as three minutes), the fact remains that this so-called fact is fictional. It seems to have become a popular 'fact' as it backs up the stereotype that men are far more sexually motivated than women and so, therefore, can be said to think of little else.

People also often back up this claim by saying the evidence can be found in the *Kinsey Report* – entitled *Sexual Behavior in the Human Male* and published in 1948 (and followed by *Sexual Behavior in the Human Female* in 1953), and was considered the authority on sexual research. However, according to the Kinsey Institute: "54% of men think about sex every day or several times a day, 43% a few times per month or a few times a week, and 4% less than once a month." Whether this is right or wrong, the *Kinsey Report* is clearly not the source for the saucy 'every seven seconds' claim.

DO TEENAGERS HAVE THE HIGHEST SUICIDE RATE?

 DO MENTHOL CIGARETTES MAKE MEN INFERTILE?

Teen angst, confusion and depression have led teenagers to be incorrectly labelled by many as the age group most likely to commit suicide. However, as a factsheet from the American National Center for Injury Prevention and Control states: "Suicide rates increase with age and are very high among those [aged] 65 years and over."

It is believed that reasons such as depression, bereavement and illness contribute to the suicidal feelings of the elderly. On the other hand, the rate of teen suicides has been steadily falling since 1992.

It's a rumour that persists despite the lack of any evidence to back it up. This is possibly based on the belief that saltpetre is used to keep the cigarettes alight, but that isn't true either.

However, there may be a glimmer of truth in the rumour, because smoking any kind of cigarettes may have an effect on a man's fertility. Researchers believe that smoking may lower a man's sperm count, and a study published in the *American Journal of Epidemiology* showed that 2.2% of non–smokers suffered from persistent impotence, compared to 3.7% of smokers.

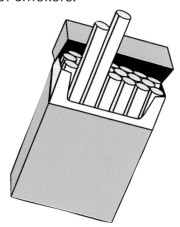

WILL EATING CRUSTS OF BREAD MAKE YOUR HAIR CURL?

It may be something that you have been told since you were a child, but there is absolutely no truth to the old wives' tale that eating the crusts of your bread will lead to a head full of ringlets and curls.

In fact, nothing you can eat will affect the curliness of your hair as this is something that is already pre-programmed into your genetic make-up. Only a date with a curling iron can change nature's plans for your locks...

 CAN YOU GET PREGNANT THE FIRST TIME YOU HAVE SEX?

Perhaps one of the most dangerous things about a lack of sex education is the rumours that fly up in its wake. Such as this particularly loathsome one that may have led more than a few young girls into an unwanted predicament.

For the record, you most certainly can get pregnant the first time you have sex. A teenage girl could even get pregnant before she has started her periods, providing her first ovulation occurs at the same time as she has intercourse; a small chance, but still a possibility. And while we're addressing these conception rumours – you can get pregnant if you have sex during your period. And jumping up and down after sex is not an effective contraceptive...

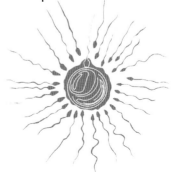

CAN YOU GET RID OF WARTS BY HAVING SOMEONE 'BUY' THEM FROM YOU?

A wonderful old wives' tale but the answer is, of course, no. Warts are caused by germs entering the skin through a cut or a scratch, causing the cells to multiply quickly.

This makes a lot of sense now, but in a less enlightened age, the sudden appearance of warts was seen as something magical and worrisome, and so a whole bunch of old wives' tales sprung up concerning warts and how to rid yourself of them.

One of these was to have someone 'buy' them from you. This was done by either the 'buyer' handing you pennies for your warts or rubbing the pennies over them. Needless to say, it does not work. And if you have hoodwinked someone into giving you money for your warts, you really should consider offering a refund...

 DO MORE PEOPLE COMMIT SUICIDE OVER THE CHRISTMAS HOLIDAY PERIOD THAN AT ANY OTHER TIME OF YEAR?

Commonly stated in films and the media, many believe the myth that suicide rates rise over the festive period of Christmas and New Year.

The typical reasons given are that people feel more lonely, that they realise that time is passing them by, or even that the despair is somehow a result of Christmas's increasing commercialism and the financial pressures of the season.

However, the myth of increased suicide rates over the holidays is – according to a 1991 study published in the *American Journal of Public Health* – just a myth. In fact, in America, suicide rates are at their lowest in the winter, and actually peak in the spring months.

DOES SUGAR MAKE CHILDREN HYPERACTIVE?

Often blamed for the hyperactive and bratty behaviour of children, sugar it seems has been unfairly treated over the years.

According to Alan Meyers, an associate professor of paediatrics at Boston University School of Medicine, eating more sugar than the recommended daily amount will not lead to any noticeable changes in a child's behaviour (although it will be very bad for their teeth).

Meyers says: "It's safe to say, based on scientific studies over the past ten years, that there is no convincing evidence that sugar intake has a negative effect on children's behaviour." His theory is also backed up by a 1994 study carried out by Vanderbilt University.

DO WOMEN HAVE MORE RIBS THAN MEN?

Stated as a scientific fact by many, the rumour that women have one rib more than men actually has its origins in the Bible, where Eve was said to be made from Adam's rib – thus depriving men of the rib, and giving it to women. However, there is no truth in the myth whatsoever.

Not only do men and women have the same number of ribs in the vast majority of cases – the number of which, by the way, is 12 – but they also almost always have the same number of ribs on each side of the body, which would not be the case if one had been taken away or added at any stage in human development.

IS SPONTANEOUS HUMAN COMBUSTION A REAL PHENOMENON?

This question has not got a simple yes or no answer. However, it does seem very unlikely that spontaneous human combustion (otherwise known as SHC) exists as a phenomenon.

Despite this, many people believe that human beings can – and do – simply burst into flames. This is said to be as a result of a chemical reaction inside the body, and is used to explain deaths where a body has been found almost totally burnt to an ash, but the furniture surrounding it is completely untouched. The main reason that sceptics have for doubting SHC is that the human body does not contain materials that burn easily.

For a start, most of the human body is water, and the only things that really burn are methane gas and body fat. These doubters point towards other explanations, such as dropped cigarettes, for the bizarre phenomenon, but there are many cases on the internet, and it is worth reading the evidence before making up your own mind.

LOCATION, LOCATION, LOCATION

Even if geography was your favourite subject at school, there are bound to be a few misconceptions that you have unknowingly fallen for. Such tall tales are covered here, along with the confusion about our solar system and natural marvels.

So, do you think you know where the tallest pyramid in the world is? Do you think half of the moon is in perpetual darkness? And can you name the world's tallest waterfall? You may have to think again! And everyone knows that water draining from a sink goes in different directions in the northern and southern hemispheres... doesn't it?

WHERE IS THE WORLD'S LARGEST PYRAMID?

Not in Egypt – surprisingly. Pyramids, although made famous for their connections with the Ancient Egyptians, also appear in other countries and cultures.

The biggest of them all is the Great Pyramid of Cholula, which can be found in Puebla, Mexico. With a base of 450m x 450m and a height of 66m, it is recognised by the *Guinness Book of Records* as the largest pyramid and the largest monument ever built.

For comparison purposes, the Great Pyramid of Cholula is almost one third larger in estimated volume than the famous Great Pyramid of Giza in Egypt, although it is not as tall.

 WHERE ARE PANAMA HATS MADE?

Panama hats are made exclusively in Ecuador. There is some debate about how they got the name 'Panama'.

Some folk say that it was because the workers who were constructing the Panama Canal wore them as protection from the searing sun. Others believe it was because the Panama Canal was used for transporting them.

Whatever the origins of the name, these wide-brimmed straw hats have been popular with top celebrities and world leaders, although their popularity diminished somewhat in the 1950s and 1960s as men stopped wearing hats so often.

IS THERE NO GRAVITY ON THE MOON?

As a matter of definition, all matter has the force of gravity as a condition of its being. However, the gravitational field of the moon has a pull that is approximately 1/6 that of the Earth's, which accounts for the astronauts being able to walk on its surface.

Isaac Newton's theory of gravity came up with an equation that relates the attraction between objects, the respective distance between the objects and the masses of the objects. In a very complex scientific way, that means that the moon does have gravity – just not as much as the Earth.

 DO INUITS HAVE HUNDREDS OF WORDS FOR SNOW?

This rumour started way back in 1911, when anthropologist Franz Boaz happened to mention that 'Eskimos have four different words for snow'.

He was referring to the Inuit people ('Eskimo' was considered a derogatory term, used by another tribe to describe the Inuits). The number of words has grown every time this 'fact' is recounted in a book or television programme, with the number now up in the hundreds.

However, linguist Steven Pinker, writing in his book *The Language Instinct*, insists: "Contrary to popular belief, the Eskimos do not have more words for snow than do speakers of English. Counting generously, experts can come up with about a dozen."

IS THE CENTRE OF THE EARTH MOLTEN ROCK?

A few misunderstandings in geography lessons at school have led to the popular misconception that the centre of the earth is bubbling hot molten rock. It is not that simple, although – like pretty much all popular misconceptions – there is a grain of truth.

The earth is made up of three main layers – the core, mantle and crust. It is the core that people believe is molten rock. However, there are two layers to the core itself, which have been named the inner and outer core. The core is made up of intensely hot iron and nickel. The inner core is solid, and the outer core is liquid.

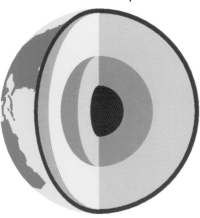

 IS ONE HALF OF THE MOON IN PERPETUAL DARKNESS?

The dark side of the moon is a famous place, where the Sun never reaches. It is cold and dark, and never seen from Earth. Right? Wrong.

There is a portion of the moon that is never seen from Earth (approximately 41%), however, it is not the gloomy place of legend. When the hemisphere of the moon that is facing us is not illuminated and the moon is new, then the so-called 'dark side' would be fully illuminated.
The reason that we only see one portion of the moon is because it rotates around on its axis during the same amount of time it takes to orbit Earth. This also refutes the popular misconception that the moon does not rotate

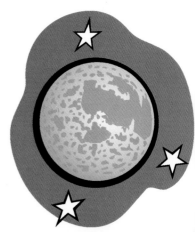

WHAT ANIMAL ARE THE CANARY ISLANDS NAMED AFTER?

WHERE ARE CHINESE GOOSEBERRIES FROM?

Although the obvious answer is that they were named after the canary, this is not in fact the case.

The Canary Islands were actually "named for canis, 'dog' for the extinct race of large dogs that once roamed the island". They were apparently named so by Pliny the Elder, who called one of the islands Canaria. He also named one island Nivaria, which means snowy. This probably referred to the snow-covered peak of Mount Teide, making Nivaria the island now known as Tenerife.

The canary is actually named so because it comes from the Canary Islands. It was named Serinus Canaria, and has been a popular pet bird in Europe since the end of the 15th century, when Spain conquered the Canary Islands.

A tricky one, this. 'Chinese gooseberries' is the name originally given to kiwi fruit – which are famously from New Zealand. However, they were known as Chinese gooseberries at first because the kiwi vine is native to south China.

It was genetically improved by the renowned New Zealand horticulturalist Hayward Wright, who developed the eponymous Hayward variety, which had its name changed from Chinese gooseberry to kiwi fruit as America in the 1950s was xenophobic, and wanted nothing to do with China.

The Chinese themselves have little interest in kiwis, except as a tonic to be given to women after they have given birth.

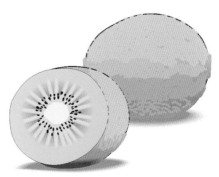

DOES THE TOILET FLUSH IN OPPOSITE DIRECTIONS IN THE NORTHERN AND SOUTHERN HEMISPHERES?

It has become 'common knowledge' that water draining from a toilet or sink will swirl in a clockwise direction in the northern hemisphere and the opposite direction in the southern hemisphere. However, this is not the case.

The effect of the Earth's spinning is known as the Coriolis force, which represents the difference in travelling speed between different points on the Earth's surface. This affects large things, such as the movement of air masses – turning them clockwise in the northern hemisphere and anticlockwise in the southern hemisphere.

However, the effect is not so large that it affects the water draining from a sink or flushing down the toilet. The construction of the sink or toilet, including the placement of taps or flush, is what actually affects the direction of the water.

WHAT IS THE TALLEST WATERFALL IN THE WORLD?

Although many would believe the answer to be Niagara Falls, this is just the most famous waterfall.

The tallest waterfall is Venezuela's 'Salto Angelo' or Angel Falls, which is 20 times higher than Niagara Falls.

Angel Falls were named after the American pilot who 'discovered' them in the 1930s. Jimmie Angel landed on a mountaintop in search of gold, and his plane ended up getting stuck. He had to walk 11 miles back to civilization, but brought with him the story of the hugely impressive waterfall he had seen.

Angel Falls are 979m high. Other impressive waterfalls are South Africa's Tugela Falls and Norway's Utigord Falls, both of which top 800m in height.

IS GREENLAND THE LARGEST ISLAND IN THE WORLD?

With a substantial area of 2,166,086km², Greenland is commonly believed to be the largest island in the world.

However, this is because many do not count Australia as an island – instead regarding it as the main part of the Australasia continent. Strictly speaking, however, with a whopping area of 7,686,850km², Australia is more than twice as big as Greenland.

Also near the top of the list are New Guinea, Borneo, Madagascar and Baffin Island (Canada). Great Britain is in the top 10, with an area of 218,100km².

IS THE GREAT WALL OF CHINA THE ONLY MAN-MADE OBJECT THAT CAN BE SEEN FROM SPACE?

This 'fact' was started well before man had even made it into space.

In reality, if you were at low orbit round the earth, you could make the Great Wall out – but you would also see thousands of other man-made structures. What's particularly amusing is that the Wall would be a fiendishly difficult structure to spot due to its colour blending in with its surroundings. Indeed, astronauts say that at a mere 180 miles up, the Great Wall is practically invisible...

However, some have even claimed that the Great Wall can be seen from the moon – but eye witnesses who have actually been to the moon say that this is absolute nonsense.

 IS THE BIG DIPPER A CONSTELLATION?

No it is not, it is an asterism – a collection of stars that make a picture but that are not recognised as a constellation. A constellation is rather like a country – it has official boundaries – rather than being a group of stars that form a picture.

The Big Dipper also goes by several other names, with 'Big Dipper' being mainly used in America. In the UK, it is known as the Plough, and Germans call it the Wagon.

During the American Civil War, slaves used the Big Dipper – which they referred to as the Drinking Gourd – to mark the way north, the way to freedom.

The Great Bear (Ursa Major) is the official name for the constellation that includes the Big Dipper.

IS THE NORTH STAR THE BRIGHTEST STAR IN THE SKY?

DO PENGUINS LIVE AT THE NORTH POLE?

Possibly the best-known star in the sky, the North Star is not, however, famous because it burns the brightest. In fact, if the Sun is included – and why not? – the North Star, also known as Polaris, ranks as the 49th brightest.

The brightest star of the night sky is the Dog Star, Sirius, which can be found below the three stars that form Orion's Belt.

The reason that the North Star is so well known is because its position in the sky makes it an excellent indicator of which way is north. However, as the Earth's axis wobbles, this was not the case 5,000 years ago and will change again in a few thousand years.

As the joke goes – why don't polar bears eat penguins? Because they can't get the wrappers off!

But seriously, it is because polar bears live at the North Pole and penguins only live in the southern hemisphere, including in Antarctica, South America, South Africa, Galapagos, Southern Australia and New Zealand.

Although the cold climate of the North Pole would be ideal for penguins just as much as the chilly South, they have never managed to cross the tropical waters and travel from South to North. And, although threatened by pollution and oil spills, there are thought to be at least 18 different species of penguins, and more than 100 million penguins worldwide.

IS THE BERMUDA TRIANGLE A CURSED PLACE FOR PLANES?

The infamous Bermuda Triangle – also known as the 'Devil's Triangle' – is roughly the area formed by making a triangle with points at Miami, Bermuda and Puerto Rico. It has gained notoriety as the place where ships and planes disappear without trace, and where air accidents are most likely to happen.

Some mystical force must be at work, some believe. For many reasons, this is simply not true. The size and location of the Bermuda Triangle varies widely, often according to the author's needs, which usually means it 'grows' to accommodate a particular incident. Also, considering the number of planes and boats that frequent the area, the rate of accidents and disappearances is not spectacular when compared with any area of the same size with the same amount of traffic.

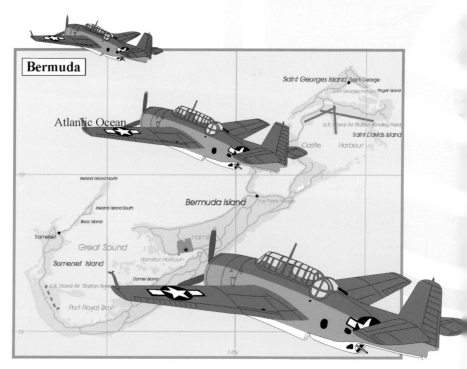

MAGNIFICENT MACHINES TERRIFYING TECHNOLOGY

The advent of complex machines and huge advances in technology have undoubtedly changed our lives for the better. However, as the nature of machines and technology is quite complicated, very few of us understand exactly what is going on inside our complex car engines or microwave ovens. Therefore, we tend to believe what we are told about these things, no matter how little basis in fact the explanation actually has.

The rules and laws concerning motoring also seem similarly confusing and vague to some, leading people to believe that they can keep points off their driving licence by overpaying a fine, or that the law requires them to surrender their vehicle if a police officer needs it to pursue a criminal. Read on, and you will soon know better!

DID THE CHEVROLET NOVA SELL BADLY IN SPANISH-SPEAKING COUNTRIES BECAUSE OF A TRANSLATION PROBLEM?

Often used as a cautionary tale, urban legend tells us that the Chevrolet Nova sold badly in Spanish-speaking countries because the word 'nova' translates as 'doesn't go'. Embarrassed officials were forced to change its name to Caribe, whereupon sales figures increased. However, although a good story, it is not at all true.

'No va' does mean 'doesn't go', but it is different to the single word 'nova' in the same way 'notable' and 'no table' would not be confused in English. Also, the car sold well in Mexico and Venezuela, allegedly two of the countries where the rumour places the poor sales figures. And finally, the Caribe was the name given to the Volkswagen Golf in Spanish–speaking countries.

 WILL A CAR'S ENGINE BE RUINED IF YOU PUT SUGAR IN THE PETROL TANK?

It has long been assumed that putting sugar in the petrol tank of a car will cause so much damage that the car will need an entirely new engine. People say that this is because the sugar dissolves in the petrol, which will then turn to sludge when heated. When cooled, this sludge will harden and stick to the engine, making i unusable.

However, sugar does not dissolve in petrol, and therefore it cannot caramelize and do the damage that popular wisdom says it can. In its granular form, sugar is as harmful as grit or sand, which are pretty common to cars, and filters are in place to prevent these things reaching the engine. A large amount of sugar could clog the filters and stop the car, but a proper clean out by a mechanic would quickly have you back on the road again.

WILL OVERPAYING A FINE KEEP POINTS OFF YOUR LICENCE?

This popular misconception has its roots in America where, people claim, you can keep points off your licence by overpaying your speeding fine by just a couple of dollars. Then, when sent a cheque made out for the difference, all that you need to do is simply not pay the cheque in.

Because the points do not go on your licence until the transaction is complete, they are therefore never going to appear as long as you hang on to that cheque. Which is a lovely idea, but entirely untrue. And neither is it true in Australia, the UK, or any of the other countries that the internet has now spread this tall tale to.

DO YOU HAVE TO SURRENDER YOUR CAR IF A POLICEMAN REQUIRES IT TO PARTICIPATE IN A CHASE?

We've all seen it in films. The policeman, in pursuit of a criminal, stops a car, pulls the driver out and takes off after the crook in their new motor. But what if you don't want to hand over your car? Is it the law that you must surrender your car if a policeman requires it?

Although laws vary the world over, not once in America or the UK has anyone been prosecuted for not handing over their car to a policeman. There is a *posse comitatus* law in some American states that requires individuals to help the police or suffer a fine, but it is unclear whether the law stretches as far as someone's property. Still, it makes for some great car chases in the movies!

CAN YOU OPEN A CAR WITH A MOBILE PHONE IF IT IS FITTED WITH A KEYLESS ENTRY SYSTEM?

 **COULD A COIN PLACED ON RAIL TRACKS CAUSE A TRAIN TO DERAIL?**

The advent of remote keyless entry for cars has led to a whole new popular misconception.

Many people believe that, should you lose your transmitting device (the thing you press to unlock the car), or leave it locked in the car with your keys, then all you need to do is ring whoever has your spare device and get them to point the device at the phone. You then hold your mobile up to the car and the vehicle will unlock! Except that it won't, as the system is not sound-based.

It's possible that OnStar has caused this confusion. As a system that can unlock your car via a cellular network, it is easy to see where the misconception came from. However, OnStar is something that is fitted into your car – there is no poor man's alternative.

Flattened coins have often been seen as a kind of good luck charm, and children have been placing them on train tracks for decades to get the desired effect. And almost all these children will have been warned at some point that their actions are potentially fatal to hundreds, as a coin on the track could cause the train to derail.

A coin on a train track has never caused a train to derail, but it has been the cause of death for those placing the coin there, or has turned the coin into a potentially lethal projectile. Two teenage girls died in 1997 when placing coins on the train tracks in Oil City, Pennsylvania. They had placed them on one set of tracks, and then stood on some other rails to watch what happened. Sadly, a train came along the track they were standing on...

And is that why airlines are so reluctant to let heavily pregnant women fly? In short, no. Research conducted reveals that most of the major carriers will not provide free air transport for life, even if you do have the good fortune to be born on one of their aircraft.

with a full educational scholarship.

Equally lucky in 1996 was Mohd Aliff Mohd Fuad, the first child to be born on an Asia Pacific Airlines flight. Due to his being the first, the airline again provided free travel and educational sponsorship.

So where did such a wacky rumour originate? Well, like all good stories, this one has its basis in fact. On two occasions, airlines have handed out travel passes for life to two lucky infants. The first was in 1995 when Dararasami Thongcharoen was born on a Thai Airways flight, two months prematurely. Not only did the lucky lady get free flights, but the airline also provided her

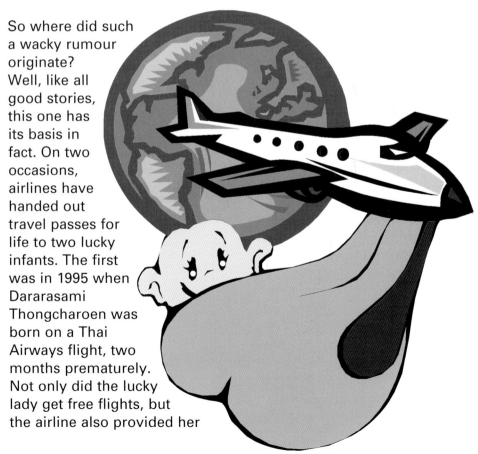

DOES SUCKING ON A PENNY BEFORE TAKING A BREATHALYZER TEST AFFECT THE READING?

It is said that sucking on a penny before blowing into a breathalyzer will render the test useless because the coin's copper coating will fool said tester.

This is nonsense. In fact, the only thing that will trick a breathalyzer test is the alcohol itself. Therefore, when a test is performed, it is important that it is done at least 20 minutes after the person being tested had a drink, otherwise the 'mouth alcohol' will interfere with the results. Some believe that burping during the test also brings the 'mouth alcohol' argument into play. Lovely.

 **COULD USING A MOBILE PHONE WHILE REFUELLING CAUSE AN EXPLOSION?**

There is no evidence that the signal from a mobile can spark off a chain of events at the pumps that will leave a neighbourhood flattened.

Urban legends such as the Australian motorist who was cooked by a fireball because he was yakking on his mobile while filling up, are nonsense – this particular tall tale was even refuted by the local fire brigade who have no record of attending such an incident. Subsequent explosions at petrol stations have all turned out to be caused by other elements.

DID MOBILE HOMES GET THEIR NAMES BECAUSE THEY CAN BE MOVED AROUND?

Many must have wondered why mobile homes are so–called, given that they are very rarely 'mobile'. True, they can be moved from place to place, but not very easily, and they are usually stationary. Their name actually refers to the town of Mobile, where the manufacture of these houses boomed.

Mobile homes were the brainchild of James and Laura Sweet as a solution to America's housing problems following the Second World War, and were originally known as Sweet Homes. However, the 1950s brought competition and many firms set up shop in the Mobile area of Alabama to take advantage of cheap labour that could be found there. Mobile homes were mass produced and well advertised, and the name stuck.

WILL STANDING AT THE BACK OF A BOAT PREVENT SEASICKNESS?

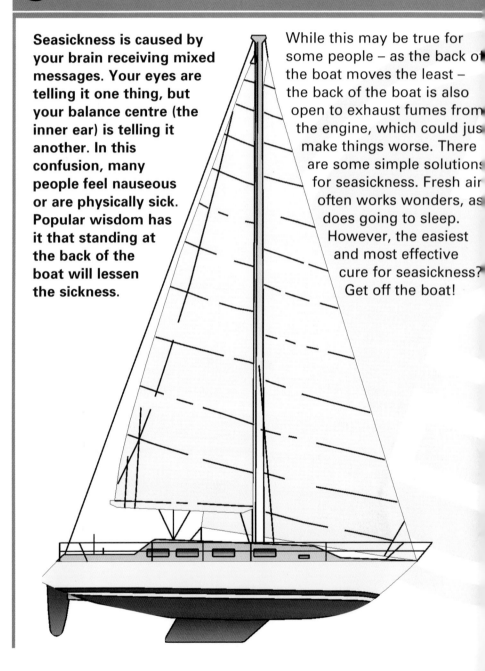

Seasickness is caused by your brain receiving mixed messages. Your eyes are telling it one thing, but your balance centre (the inner ear) is telling it another. In this confusion, many people feel nauseous or are physically sick. Popular wisdom has it that standing at the back of the boat will lessen the sickness.

While this may be true for some people – as the back of the boat moves the least – the back of the boat is also open to exhaust fumes from the engine, which could just make things worse. There are some simple solutions for seasickness. Fresh air often works wonders, as does going to sleep. However, the easiest and most effective cure for seasickness? Get off the boat!

POP CULTURE & MODERN MYTHS

Modern life has produced many popular misconceptions that have sprung up from all kinds of sources. The world of movies is a rich source of misquotes and misconceptions, while literature and television also play their part.

From Bogart's famous line that he never said in *Casablanca*, to Michael Caine's never-uttered catchphrase and Dorothy's ruby slippers, there are bound to be 'facts' in this section whose revelation as complete works of fiction will surprise you.

Also featured here are the modern myths about day-to-day life that have assumed the status of urban legend, and that people still continue to believe.

CAN YOU CLEAR DEBTS BY MAKING OUT A CHEQUE FOR A FRACTION OF THE AMOUNT OWED AND WRITING 'PAID IN FULL' ON IT?

A popular myth that has long been doing the rounds is the one that says writing a cheque for a fraction of the amount owed will clear a large debt, provided that it has a note saying 'paid in full' attached to it. This is not true, and will probably be seen as acting in bad faith, which will just make things worse.

The rumour may have popped up as a result of some creditors being willing to accept a smaller amount than that originally owed – after all, some payment is better than no payment – but this only works when there is an agreement between creditor and debtor.

DID HUMPHREY BOGART SAY, "PLAY IT AGAIN, SAM" IN THE FILM CASABLANCA?

Casablanca – made in 1942 and starring Humphrey Boga and Ingrid Bergman – is one the most quoted films in history. Gems such as, "Here lookin' at you, kid", "We'll always have Paris" and "Of a the gin joints, in all the town in all the world, she had to walk into mine", have worke their way into the public consciousness over the years

However, perhaps the most famous of all the lines to con from the film – Bogart saying "Play it again, Sam" – was never actually said. Bergman says, "Play it once, Sam" in reference to the song *As Tim Goes By*, and Bogart says, "If she can stand it, I can! Play it Public memory has neatened this quote so that it is easy to remember, despite the fact that neither of them ever said it.

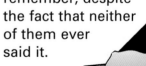

DOES DOROTHY WEAR RUBY SLIPPERS IN THE ORIGINAL WIZARD OF OZ?

DID SHERLOCK HOLMES SAY "ELEMENTARY, MY DEAR WATSON"?

Now firmly ensconced in the public memory is the image of Dorothy clicking her heels together three times and repeating the words: "There's no place like home". And on those feet are the famous ruby slippers. Right?

Well, if you're watching the 1935 film starring Judy Garland as Dorothy, then there are indeed ruby slippers. However, in the original book by L Frank Baum, Dorothy wears silver slippers. The film version used silver slippers at first, until MGM studio chief Louis B Mayer realised that red would photograph much better in Technicolor, and so the shoes were changed.

Garland wore several pairs of ruby slippers during filming, which are now highly prized by collectors of movie memorabilia, and each pair is valued at an approximate $1.5 million.

Despite entering into the public awareness as a well-known catchphrase, nowhere in the 60 Sherlock Holmes stories by Sir Arthur Conan Doyle does the legendary detective utter the phrase: "Elementary, my dear Watson".

He does often use the word "elementary" to describe his conclusions, but not once does he use the famous phrase in full. "Elementary, my dear Watson" appears for the first time at the end of *The Return of Sherlock Holmes*, the first Sherlock Holmes sound film made, in 1929.

HOW DID HARRY HOUDINI DIE?

There are several rumours concerning the death of master magician Ehrich Weiss – better known as Harry Houdini. However, the truth is that he died on October 31, 1926 of peritonitis caused by appendicitis.

The 1953 movie *Houdini*, starring Tony Curtis, depicts the illusionist dying when a trick goes wrong and he drowns in the infamous Chinese water torture cell. Although this is untrue, some still regard it as fact.

Another rumour is that Houdini died from a punch to the stomach. Houdini was well known for withstanding blows to the abdomen by tensing his muscles. It is said that a student challenged him without warning, therefore not giving him time to tense his muscles. Although it is possible that this blow ruptured his appendix, it could not have been the cause of his fatal appendicitis, as this is a bacterial infection.

 DID MICHAEL CAINE SAY, "NOT A LOT OF PEOPLE KNOW THAT" IN THE FILM ALFIE?

Perhaps due to his charming Cockney accent, Michael Caine is one of the film world's most mimicked men. However the phrase, "not a lot of people know that" was not only not spoken by Caine in the 1966 film *Alfie*, but he never uttered the words at all except when mocking himself in later years.

Peter Sellers is the source of the catchphrase, when he recorded an answerphone message doing a scarily good impression of Caine. The message said: "My name is Michael Caine. Peter Sellers is not in at the moment. Not a lot of people know that."

IS GROUND GLASS A DEADLY MURDER WEAPON?

In many murder mysteries and television dramas, ground glass has been used as an effective murder weapon.

The killer simply needs to grind up the glass, mix it in with the victim's food, and then sit back and wait for internal bleeding to do the rest. However, the murderer will be waiting for some time, as ingesting ground glass is not deadly. The glass would have to be very finely crushed, otherwise the intended victim would notice the texture in his food, as is noted by Dr DP Lyle in his book *Murder and Mayhem* (2003): "Salt dissolves but glass doesn't, so the food would seem gritty unless the glass was ground into a powder. But very fine glass is unlikely to cause any lethal damage to the GI tract. It would be more of an irritation, with minor bleeding if any at all."

DID CLINT EASTWOOD SAY, "DO YOU FEEL LUCKY, PUNK?" IN THE FILM DIRTY HARRY?

It's a great line to sneer out of the corner of your mouth, but in reality, what Clint Eastwood actually said in the 1971 film *Dirty Harry* was a little more long-winded.

Eastwood plays Inspector Harry Callahan, who has a suspect at gunpoint and delivers the following speech: "I know what you're thinking. 'Did he fire six shots or only five?' Well, to tell you the truth, in all this excitement I kinda lost track myself. But being as this is a .44 Magnum, the most powerful handgun in the world, and would blow your head clean off, you've got to ask yourself a question. 'Do I feel lucky?' Well, do ya, punk?"

CAN A PRISONER GO FREE IF THE FIRST ATTEMPT TO EXECUTE HIM FAILS?

It's a popular misconception that has been helped by films and television – if an attempt to hang a prisoner fails, then said prisoner automatically earns a reprieve and can go free. This myth has also been applied to the electric chair, the guillotine and the firing squad methods of execution.

It is possible that this belief originated with the idea that divine intervention would prevent the execution of an innocent man. However, it is not true. The sentence received by the prisoner would always read 'until dead'; for example 'to be hanged by the neck until dead', so the sentence would still be carried out if the rope was to break.

However, some people argue that to subject a man to further execution attempts after the first has failed falls into the category of 'cruel and unusual punishment'.

 WILL PEEING IN A PUBLIC POOL LEAVE YOU BLUSHING?

It's a widely held belief that if you pee in a public pool, then a special "urine-indicator" dye will activate and leave the water round you as bright red as your resulting complexion.

This is simply not true – there is no such dye in use because no one has yet to figure out how to make a dye that will detect only urine. The myth perpetuates to this day though as the ultimate deterrent to halt the 'leaking' bladders of children, by threatening them with complete and instant humiliation. Not any more though!

DID MAE WEST SAY, "COME UP AND SEE ME SOMETIME"?

In the 1933 film *She Done Him Wrong*, Mae West is commonly believed to have spoken the ultimate seduction line, "Come up and see me sometime".

However, this is a case of the public memory neatening up a line that wasn't quite as snappy. What West really said was, "Why don't you come up sometime 'n' see me?"

However, despite being misquoted on this occasion, Mae West was queen of the one-liner, giving us such classics as, "Is that a gun in your pocket, or are you just glad to see me?" and "It's not the men in my life that counts – it's the life in my men".

ARE DOCTORS REQUIRED TO TAKE THE HIPPOCRATIC OATH?

The Hippocratic Oath is something that doctors in training swear by at medical school. It involves certain rules about being a doctor, such as patient confidentiality and the phrase, "first, do no harm". Right? Wrong!

The original Hippocratic Oath is rarely used anywhere as it has been changed and modified as the practice of medicine has changed over the years. The original mentions not practising abortion, which is certainly not sworn by doctors today.

And the phrase "first, do no harm" is not included in the Hippocratic Oath, although probably stems from Hippocrates' Epidemics, which reads: "Declare the past, diagnose the present, foretell the future; practice these acts. As to diseases, make a habit of two things – to help, or at least do no harm."

DO STUDENTS AUTOMATICALLY PASS THE YEAR IF THEIR UNIVERSITY ROOMMATE COMMITS SUICIDE?

Or if someone kills themselves during an exam? Such stories frequently make the rounds of university dorms on both sides of the Atlantic. In America, it is said that a student will receive a 4.0 average for the year if their roommate dies – this covers murder or suicide (although, not presumably if you were to kill your own roommate). So, is it true?

No, it is not. There is not one American university with the policy to award a 4.0 average as compensation for suffering a traumatic experience, and no university in the UK or USA has given grades because of witnessing an exam–room suicide.

Indeed, there have been no reports of anyone committing suicide during an exam.

 DID JAMES CAGNEY SAY, "YOU DIRTY RAT"?

Despite being famous for his gangster characters in films and sneering, "You dirty rat" before blowing someone's brains out, Cagney was actually a talented song and dance man, who never actually uttered the words, "You dirty rat" in a film.

The misconception probably sprung up from Cagney's appearance in the 1931 film *Taxi*, when he uttered the line: "Come out and take it, you dirty, yellow-bellied rat, or I'll give it to you through the door."

When the American Film Institute saluted James Cagney in 1974, the actor himself set the record straight in his acceptance speech, saying: "I never said, 'You dirty rat'."

DID CAPTAIN KIRK SAY "BEAM ME UP, SCOTTY"?

Throughout all the seasons of *Star Trek* and the following films, not once did William Shatner's Captain Kirk say the infamous words, "Beam me up, Scotty".

He said something similar – "Kirk to Enterprise. Beam us up, Scotty" – on the 1973 animated *Star Trek* show, but never in the show itself.

Patrick Stewart, however, did say the line when playing Captain Picard in *Star Trek: The Next Generation*. Despite the phrase never being used in the original series, it has truly made its mark in popular culture, becoming well known even with those who aren't fans of the programme.

DID SPOCK SAY "IT'S LIFE, JIM, BUT NOT AS WE KNOW IT"?

Another famous *Star Trek* 'quote' that was never uttered in the television show, or in any of the films. The line "It's life, Jim, but not as we know it" was actually taken from a 1987 pop song *Star Trekkin'* by The Firm. Spock – the character famously played by Leonard Nimoy – never said the words.

That song also contains the line "It's worse than that, he's dead, Jim", which people presume was said by Doctor 'Bones' McCoy, the Starship Enterprise's doctor, played by DeForest Kelley. However, what he said was simply, "He's dead, Jim."

However, the other famous *Star Trek* quote "To boldly go where no man has gone before" certainly was said by William Shatner's Captain Kirk.

IS WALT DISNEY'S BODY CRYOGENICALLY FROZEN?

Since he died in 1966, rumours about Walt Disney's desire to be cryogenically frozen have abounded. The earliest known published account was in 1969, and many books have repeated the rumour as fact.

On some level it makes sense. Walt Disney was certainly very interested in looking to the future – the 'Community of Tomorrow' EPCOT Center was a project he was personally very involved in – and he was seen as something of an innovator. However, the fact remains that Walt Disney is not cryogenically frozen. His death certificate confirms that he was cremated and interred in Forest Lawn Memorial Park, Glendale.

Disney's daughter Diane addressed the rumour in 1972, writing: "There is absolutely no truth to the rumour that my father, Walt Disney, wished to be frozen. I doubt that my father had ever heard of cryonics."